SAVING THE PLANET THROUGH GREEN ENERGY

GEOTHERMAL ENERGY

COLIN GRADY

Enslow Publishing
101 W. 23rd Street
Suite 240
New York, NY 10011
USA

enslow.com

Published in 2017 by Enslow Publishing, LLC.
101 W. 23rd Street, Suite 240, New York, NY 10011

Library of Congress Cataloging-in-Publication Data
Names: Grady, Colin.
Title: Geothermal energy / Colin Grady.
Description: New York, NY: Enslow Publishing, 2017. | Series: Saving the Planet Through Green Energy | Includes bibliographical references and index.
Identifiers: LCCN 2016021784| ISBN 9780766082823 (library bound) | ISBN 9780766082809 (pbk.) | ISBN 9780766082816 (6-pack)
Subjects: LCSH: Geothermal engineering—Juvenile literature.
Classification: LCC TJ280.7 .G68 2016 | DDC 621.44—dc23
LC record available at https://lccn.loc.gov/2016021784

Printed in China

To Our Readers: We have done our best to make sure all website addresses in this book were active and appropriate when we went to press. However, the author and the publisher have no control over and assume no liability for the material available on those websites or on any websites they may link to. Any comments or suggestions can be sent by e-mail to customerservice@enslow.com.

Portions of this book originally appeared in the book *Geothermal Energy: Hot Stuff!* by Amy S. Hansen.

Photos Credits: Cover, p. 1 Universal Images Group/Getty Images (geothermal plant); Mad Dog/Shutterstock.com (series logo and chapter openers); p. 7 Pyty/Shutterstock.com; p. 8 Lukiyanova Natalia/frenta/Shutterstock.com; p. 10 Kenneth Keifer/Shutterstock.com; p. 11 Sura Ark/Moment Mobile /Getty Images; p. 15 Fouad A. Saad/Shutterstock.com; p. 16 Mat Hayward/Shutterstock.com; p. 18 MyLoupe/Universal Images Group/Getty Images; p. 19 Dmcdevit/Wikimedia Commons/public domain/Geothermal heat map US.png; p. 22 Thomas Koehler/Photothek/Getty Images.

CONTENTS

WORDS TO KNOW

ancestors Relatives who lived long ago.

cycle Actions that happen in the same order over and over.

engineers Masters at planning and building engines, machines, roads, and bridges.

erupts Breaks open.

furnaces Things in which heat is produced.

generated Made.

geysers Springs that send up jets of hot water or steam.

greenhouses Buildings that trap heat to make it warm enough to grow plants.

pressurized Under a force that pushes things together.

temperature How hot or cold something is.

turbines Motors that turn by a flow of water or air.

CHAPTER 1
HEAT FROM UNDER THE GROUND

What is geothermal energy? It is the heat that comes from inside Earth. It is warmer deeper under ground, thanks to Earth's geothermal energy. Black ants know all about this! When the cold winter weather is coming, they move their nests deeper under the ground. They do this so that they do not freeze. If you go about 10 feet (3 meters) down, the ground stays between 50 and 60° F (10–16° C). If you dig even deeper, you will find the **temperature** getting warmer and warmer.

People use geothermal energy to heat or cool buildings and to make electricity. Geothermal energy is a rather clean energy source. We do not pollute when we use it. Geothermal energy is also renewable. That means we cannot use it up.

ENERGY FROM EARTH'S LAYERS

There are places on Earth where heat escapes as hot steam. Geothermal energy can be used as a clean energy source.

Earth has three layers. They are the crust, mantle, and core. The core is at Earth's center. This is the hottest layer. It is still hot from when Earth formed, more than four billion years ago. Much of Earth's heat is **generated** in the core and flows out to the mantle, Earth's middle layer.

GEOTHERMAL ENERGY

The mantle contains melted rocks, called magma. Magma heats up water deep under ground. When water reaches Earth's crust, or outside layer, it causes hot springs and **geysers**. This superheated water can be used to make electricity. It also powers geothermal energy systems. Earth's crust is warmed by the sun. We use energy from the crust for geothermal energy systems called geothermal heat pumps.

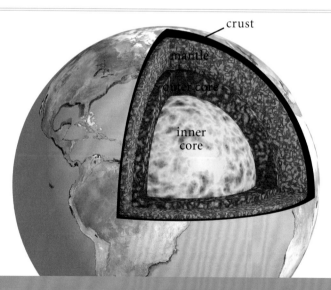

crust

mantle

outer core

inner core

The magma in Earth's mantle heats up underground water. This very hot water can be used for energy.

CHAPTER 2

HARNESSING HEAT FROM HOT WATER

There are as many as five hundred geysers at Yellowstone National Park. They shoot hot water into the air. Long before there was a park, early Native Americans used these geysers. They cooked food and bathed in the hot water. Other ancient people used hot springs and geysers, too. The ancient Chinese and Japanese built baths around hot springs. The ancient Romans piped hot water out of hot springs and into their bathtubs.

In 1904, Italians went beyond what their Roman **ancestors** had done. They created the first geothermal power plant. The plant used steam that rose out of holes in the ground to make electricity.

Native Americans used geysers, like this one at Yellowstone National Park, to cook food and take baths.

PUTTING HOT WATER TO WORK

If you live near a hot spring, it is not hard to come up with uses for the hot water. For example, the people of Reykjavík, Iceland, use their hot springs to heat buildings. The hot springs are many miles away, so a pipeline carries the water to the city, where it is stored. They pipe hot water from the storage tanks into nearby buildings for heat.

Geothermal energy can also help plants grow. Farmers build **greenhouses** that use geothermal energy in some places where farming is hard. Inside the greenhouses, there are pipes full of hot water drawn up from under the ground. The hot water warms both the soil and the air inside the building. People use this method to grow vegetables in Hungary, Italy, Iceland, and New Mexico.

A greenhouse in Iceland uses geothermal heating to grow flowers.

GEOTHERMAL ENERGY TIMELINE

4 billion years ago Earth forms as a fiery ball. It begins to cool off slowly.

10,000 years ago Early Native Americans cook and bathe in the geysers in what is now Yellowstone National Park.

79 CE Mount Vesuvius **erupts**. It destroys the geothermal-heated Roman baths in Pompeii, Italy.

1892 **Engineers** in Boise, Idaho, use hot springs to heat local buildings.

1904 Engineers in Lardello, Italy, make electricity with the first geothermal power generator.

1948 Carl Nielsen builds the first geothermal heat pump in his home in Ohio.

1960 Pacific Gas and Electric starts the first large dry steam power plant in the United States, at the Geysers, in California.

1974 Engineers in Los Alamos, New Mexico, start working with hot dry rock electricity systems.

1980 Brawley, California, becomes home to the first US flash power plant.

1981 The first binary geothermal power plant begins producing energy in Raft River, Idaho.

2005 The Energy Policy Act of 2005 becomes US law, making geothermal energy more competitive with fossil fuels for making electricity.

2015 The amount of electricity able to be made by geothermal power in the world rises to 12.8 gigawatts (GW). That is enough to power more than four million homes for one year.

CHAPTER 3

MAKING ELECTRICITY

A power plant is a place where electricity is made. Most of these plants use energy to heat water to very high temperatures, which creates steam. When the steam rises, it turns **turbines**, which make electricity. This is easy with geothermal power plants since most of them start out with superheated hot water.

There are several kinds of geothermal plants. In flash steam plants, engineers pipe hot, **pressurized** water from under the ground to the surface. When they lower the pressure, the water turns to steam, or flashes. In binary power plants, engineers use hot water to boil a liquid that creates steam to turn turbines.

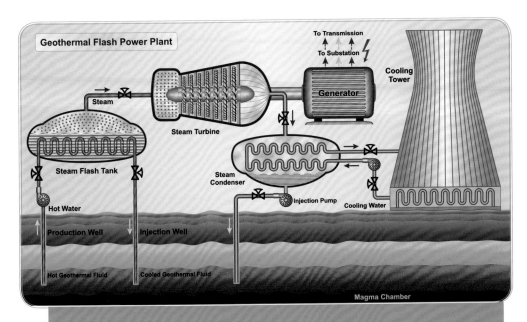

Geothermal Flash Power Plant

To Transmission

To Substation

Steam

Steam Turbine

Cooling Tower

Generator

Steam Flash Tank

Steam Condenser

Hot Water

Injection Pump

Cooling Water

Production Well

Injection Well

Hot Geothermal Fluid

Cooled Geothermal Fluid

Magma Chamber

In geothermal power plants, hot water from under the ground can be turned into steam. The steam turns the turbines to make electricity.

ELECTRICITY WITH DRY ROCKS

There are places where there is underground heat but no nearby water. Engineers are finding ways to bring water to these hot spots. Then people will be able to use the geothermal energy there. Hot dry rock, or HDR, systems are one way to do this.

Scientists in Los Alamos, New Mexico, began building the first HDR system in 1970. The system used three wells, each about 2 miles (3 km) deep. Engineers sent cold water down the first well. The cold water hit the hot rocks and broke them. The water turned hot. Some of it turned to steam. The steam and water then rose up through the other wells and turned turbines.

Cell phones and other devices need electricity. When geothermal energy is used to make the electricity, there is less pollution to the planet.

CHAPTER 4

HEATING HOMES AND BUILDINGS

Making electricity is one use for Earth's heat. Engineers have also found ways to heat buildings with heat from Earth's crust when there is no water source. They use a heat pump to capture geothermal energy.

A heat pump starts by moving water through the ground. The water warms up. The warm water heats a gas called Freon. Next, the hot Freon enters a machine called a compressor. The compressor presses the gas into a smaller area. This makes the gas even hotter. A fan blows air over the hot Freon. The air warms up and is used to heat the building. In time, the compressor lets the Freon out. The gas cools off, and the **cycle** starts again.

WHY DOESN'T EVERYONE USE GEOTHERMAL ENERGY?

One of the biggest problems with geothermal power plants is that not everyone can use them. Geothermal power plants make clean energy, but they have to be built near a source of geothermal heat. Or in the case of Iceland, the water must be pumped to the larger cities. In North America, most of those sources are in the West.

Pipes for a geothermal heating system are placed in the ground. The pipes help bring heat to a home.

Milliwatts (thermal)
per square meter

> 100
80 - 100
60 - 80
40 - 60
< 40

The colors on this United States map show the underground temperature up to 4 miles (6 km) deep. The darkest red areas are the hottest; the light blue areas are the coolest. You can see that the warmest areas are in the West.

A second problem is that engineers find that some geothermal power plants run out of steam. They are fixing this problem by adding more water. For example, the city of Santa Rosa, California, pipes its cleaned wastewater to a group of geothermal plants called the Geysers. The water keeps the power plants working.

A third problem is that the water that rises to the surface is not necessarily pure. Many times it contains salts and has to be treated before it is used.

CHAPTER 5

THE FUTURE OF GEOTHERMAL ENERGY

Power from geothermal energy is reliable and kind to our planet. It is also cost effective. Some countries, such as the Philippines, make more than a quarter of their electricity from geothermal heat. Geothermal energy use is becoming more and more common. Some new schools use geothermal heat pumps instead of **furnaces** or air conditioners. Farmers can keep fish in ponds warmed by geothermal heat. Running pipes of warm water under sidewalks can keep them clear of snow.

Engineers are now looking for ways to get more energy from Earth. They are

Steam from a geothermal power plant is used to make electricity. The more heat we can use from Earth, the less we will need to use fossil fuels.

experimenting with drilling deeper to collect more heat. They are finding places where magma can be easily reached. Back in 2007, twenty-four countries used geothermal heat to make electricity. Today, that number is growing!

FURTHER READING

BOOKS

Bow, James. *Energy from Earth's Core: Geothermal Energy.* New York, NY: Crabtree Publishing Co., 2016.

Britcher, Angela. *The Pros and Cons of Geothermal Power.* New York, NY: Cavendish Square, 2016.

Centore, Michael. *Renewable Energy.* Broomall, PA: Mason Crest, 2015.

Doeden, Matt. *Finding Out About Geothermal Energy.* Minneapolis, MN: Lerner Publications Co., 2015.

Kopp, Megan. *Living in a Sustainable Way: Green Communities.* New York, NY: Crabtree Publishing Co., 2016.

Sneideman, Joshua. *Renewable Energy: Discover the Fuel of the Future with 20 Projects.* White River Junction, VT: Nomad Press, 2016.

WEBSITES

Energy Star Kids
energystar.gov/index.cfm?c=kids.kids_index
Learn more facts about energy and how you can save energy and help the planet.

NASA's Climate Kids: Energy
climatekids.nasa.gov/menu/energy
Lots of fun facts and links about energy.

US Energy Information Administration
eia.gov/kids
Read about the history of energy, get facts about the types of energy, learn tips to save energy, and link to games and activities.

INDEX